W9-CYG-927

SPORTING CHAMPIONSHIPS
NCAA BASKETBALL CHAMPIONSHIP

Annalise Bekkering

WEIGL PUBLISHERS INC.

Published by Weigl Publishers Inc.
350 5th Avenue, Suite 3304, PMB 6G
New York, NY 10118-0069

Website: www.weigl.com

Library of Congress Cataloging-in-Publication Data

Bekkering, Annalise.
 NCAA Basketball Championship/ Annalise Bekkering.
    p. cm. -- (Sporting championships)
Includes bibliographical references and index.
 ISBN 978-1-60596-634-2 (hard cover : alk. paper) -- ISBN 978-1-60596-635-9 (soft cover : alk. paper)
1. National Collegiate Athletic Association--Juvenile literature. 2. Women's National Basketball Association--Juvenile literature. I. Title.
 GV885.3.B45 2010
 796.323082--dc22
 [B]
                                        2009008366
Printed in China
1 2 3 4 5 6 7 8 9 0 13 12 11 10 09

Weigl acknowledges Getty Images as its primary image supplier for this title.

Project Coordinator
Heather C. Hudak

Design
Terry Paulhus

All of the Internet URLs given in the book were valid at the time of publication. However, due to the dynamic nature of the Internet, some addresses may have changed, or sites may have ceased to exist since publication. While the author and publisher regret any inconvenience this may cause readers, no responsibility for any such changes can be accepted by either the author or the publisher.

Every reasonable effort has been made to trace ownership and to obtain permission to reprint copyright material. The publishers would be pleased to have any errors or omissions brought to their attention so that they may be corrected in subsequent printings.

CONTENTS

30

What is the NCAA Basketball Championship?

Each year, university basketball teams from all over the United States compete for a chance to play in the final game of the National **Collegiate** Athletic Association (NCAA) basketball championship. Winning the championship is **prestigious**, and the final game is one of the most popular sporting events in the United States.

The NCAA is an organization that oversees most college and university sports in the United States. More than 1,000 schools are members of the NCAA. Member schools are divided into three divisions. Division I is made up of the largest schools. These schools offer many sports programs. Division II and Division III schools are smaller. All three divisions host championship games, but the Division I championship is the most popular.

Blake Griffin of the Oklahoma Sooners was a top college player before deciding to enter the National Basketball Association (NBA) draft in 2009.

All of the athletes that compete in the NCAA are students. They have athletic and academic responsibilities to maintain. Athletes must achieve high grades to be able to play sports for their school.

CHANGES THROUGHOUT THE YEARS	
PAST	**PRESENT**
In 1939, there was an audience of 5,500 people for the final game.	In 2008, attendance at the final game was 43,257.
In 1977, the average ticket price was $7.78.	In 2008, the average ticket price was $77.92.
In 1946, 500,000 people watched the final game on television.	In 2008, more than 19.5 million people watched the championship game on television.

Trophies

The winning team of the NCAA championship receives two different trophies. One is a gold-plated National Championship trophy awarded by the NCAA. The other trophy is from the National Association of Basketball Coaches. It is made out of Waterford crystal and is shaped like a basketball.

NCAA Basketball History

Dr. James Naismith invented basketball in 1891, in Springfield, Massachusetts. He developed the game as an indoor activity for students to take part in during the winter. The game was played with a soccer ball and peach baskets that were hung on each end of the gymnasium. Players would climb up a ladder to retrieve the ball from the baskets. Eventually, the bottom of the baskets was cut out so the ball would fall to the ground.

The head of the physical education department gave Dr. James Naismith 14 days to invent an indoor sport.

Basketball became popular very quickly. The first college game was played in 1896, when the University of Chicago beat the University of Iowa 15 to 12. By 1900, about 90 colleges in the United States had basketball teams.

In 1906, the Intercollegiate Athletic Association of the United States (IAAUS) formed to regulate college sports. Four years later, it became the National Collegiate Athletic Association (NCAA). More the 360 colleges had basketball teams by 1914.

In 1946, Oklahoma A&M beat out North Carolina in the championship game. They only won by three points.

In 1937, Kansas City, Missouri, hosted what was meant to be the first national college basketball tournament. However, all of the teams came from the midwest rather than from across the nation. In 1938, the National Invitational Tournament (NIT) held its first event. Though the event took place in New York, it received attention across the country. The first NCAA tournament was held the following year. It was organized by the National Association of Basketball Coaches (NABC) in an effort to draw more attention to the sport in the western states. The NCAA took over the tournament the next year.

At first, both NIT and NCAA tournaments were popular. The NCAA championship later became the ultimate college basketball tournament.

For the first 12 years, the NCAA divided the country into eight districts, and one team from each participated in the NCAA championship tournaments. As the tournament increased in popularity, it gradually grew to include 65 teams. Today, the NCAA basketball championship, commonly called March Madness, is one of the biggest and most-watched sporting events in the United States.

Basketball Cheers

Basketball fans have different chants and cheers for their favorite teams. Many of these cheers have been part of the sport for a long time and are a tradition for the team. One of the best-known cheers comes from the students at Kansas University. At home games, when the Jayhawks win, hundreds of fans chant "Rock, Chalk! Jayhawk! KU!"

Rules of the Game

Basketball rules have changed very little since the sport was invented in 1891. Though some leagues throughout the world have different rules, the game is essentially the same wherever it is played.

1 The Game

In NCAA basketball, the game is made up of two halves that are 20 minutes long each. There is a 15-minute break between halves. This is called the halftime. The team with the highest score at the end of the game wins. If the score is tied at the end of the game, the teams play five minutes of overtime. Each team is allowed five players on the court at once. These five players play **offense** and **defense**.

2 Beginning the Game

Every basketball game begins with a jump ball. A player from each team faces off at center court. The other players line up around the circle at half court. A referee tosses the ball in the air between the two players that are facing each other, and they try to knock the ball toward one of their teammates around the circle.

3 Moving the Ball

There are two ways to move the basketball around the court. These are dribbling and passing. Dribbling is done by bouncing the ball against the floor. Players are not allowed to carry the ball while moving their feet, so they must dribble the ball. If a player takes a step while holding the ball, the referee will call a traveling violation. Passing, or tossing the ball to another player on the same team, is a fast way to move the ball around the court. Basketball players need to have good passing skills. They need to prevent the other team's players from catching the passes they throw.

4 Scoring

On offense, a team scores points by shooting the ball into the basket. The team scores two points for a shot taken close to the hoop and three points for a shot from behind the **three-point line**. In NCAA basketball, the offensive team has 35 seconds to shoot the ball at the net. While on defense, the other team tries to prevent the offense from scoring. To do this, they block shots and passes, and try to take control of the ball.

5 Fouls

A foul occurs when there is illegal contact between players, such as pushing, tripping, or holding, during play. If a defensive player fouls an offensive player during a shot, the offensive player gets to shoot foul shots at the basket. The player gets to stand at a special place on the court in front of the basket, called the free-throw line. Each time the ball makes it through the hoop on a foul shot, the team gets one point. A player can also get a technical foul for unsportsmanlike behavior.

Making the Call

In NCAA basketball games, there are three referees. Referees make sure that players are following the rules and that the game is fair. A referee must have extensive knowledge of the rules of basketball. When a rule is broken, the referee stops the game by blowing a whistle. Referees run up and down the court to follow and watch the players. A referee must be able to make decisions very quickly.

The Basketball Court

Basketball is played on a rectangular court that is 94 feet (28.7 meters) long by 50 feet (15.2 m) wide. There is a basket in the center of each end of the court. The basket is 18 inches (45.7 centimeters) in diameter. The backboard behind the basket is 4 feet (1.2 m) high by 6 feet (1.8 m) wide.

At each end of the court, there is a rectangular box drawn on the floor, with the basket at one end. This box measures 19 feet (5.8 m) long by 12 feet (3.7 m) wide. This area is called the key. Offensive players are only allowed to stand in the key for three seconds. The free-throw line at the top of the key is 13 feet (3.9 m) from the basket.

The three-point line in NCAA basketball is an **arced** line 19 feet 9 inches (6 m) from the basket. Any shot made from behind this line is worth three points.

Basketball can be played on many different surfaces. For outdoor games, it can be played on asphalt or concrete. In gymnasiums and arenas, basketball courts most often have hardwood floors. Some indoor courts are made out of flexible, interlocking tiles.

Players on the Team

Each basketball team has five players on the court at one time. Each member of the team has different strengths and skills. All teammates play both offense and defense. On offense, the point guard is usually small and fast, and has excellent ball handling and passing skills. The shooting guard is often very quick, and is good at scoring and passing. The small forward is good at scoring both near and far from the net. The power forward is normally big and strong. This player needs strong defensive and **rebounding** skills. The center is usually the tallest player on the team. Centers score many points near the net and block shots on defense. The coach is an important part of the team. This person is in charge of strategy and instructing players.

THE BASKETBALL COURT

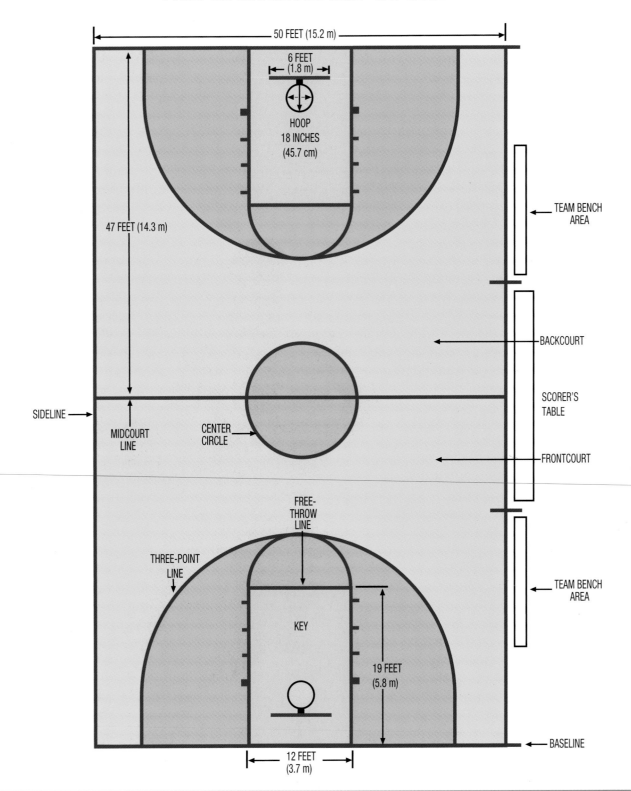

Basketball Equipment

Playing basketball requires very little equipment. This is one of the reasons that it is such a popular sport. People of different ages and skill levels can play it indoors or outdoors, on many different surfaces.

The most important piece of equipment is a basketball. Most often, the ball is made of nylon or leather and is orange or brown in color. The surface of the ball is pebbled. This rough surface allows players to grip the ball better. A men's basketball is 29.5 to 30 inches (74.9 to 76.2 cm) in **circumference** and weighs 20 to 22 ounces (567 to 624 grams). It is slightly larger than a women's basketball, which is 28.5 to 29 inches (72.4 to 73.7 cm) in circumference and weighs 17.5 to 19.5 ounces (496 to 553 grams).

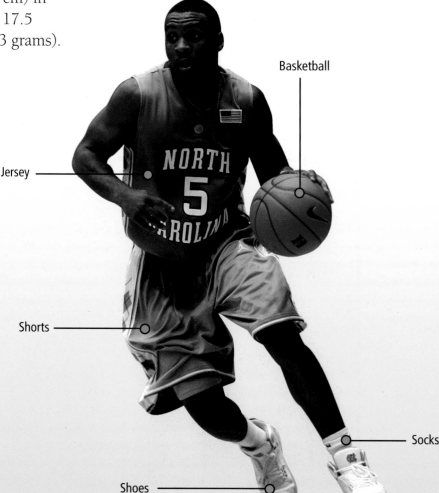

Basketball

Jersey

NORTH CAROLINA 5

Shorts

Socks

Shoes

GET CONNECTED

To learn more about basketball equipment and rules, visit **http://entertainment. howstuffworks.com/ basketball.htm.**

Most players wear high-top shoes. Basketball players move around a great deal and make quick movements side-to-side. Having high-top shoes helps prevent players from injuring their ankles.

The basket is another important piece of equipment in basketball. The rim is made out of metal and has a diameter of 18 inches (45.7 cm). The net below is made from nylon. In outdoor basketball, the net is sometimes made out of chains. The basket is attached to a backboard made of wood or glass. Players try to bounce the ball off the backboard at angles to get the ball to fall into the basket.

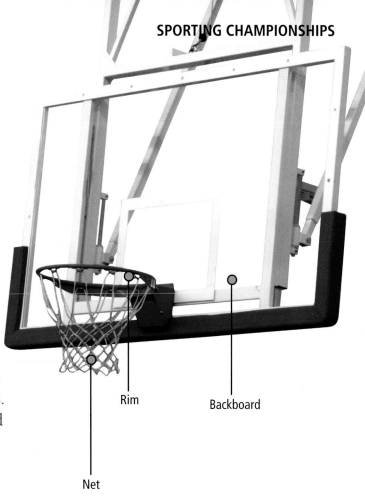

Rim

Backboard

Net

Team Uniforms

Most basketball uniforms consist of a sleeveless top and shorts in the team's colors. The uniforms are made out of synthetic, or humanmade, materials, such as nylon, polyester, or rayon. Players have a number on the front and back of their uniform. In the NCAA, the players can have the numbers 00, 0 to 15, 20 to 25, 30 to 35, 40 to 45, or 50 to 55. Sometimes, the player's last name is written on the back of the uniform above the number. In the NCAA, each team has a light-colored uniform and a dark-colored uniform. The home team wears the light uniform, and the visiting team wears the dark uniform.

Qualifying to Play

The Division I final tournament is called the Final Four. The road to the Final Four takes place over three weeks in March and April every year. Sixty-five teams qualify for the NCAA championship tournament. The selection of these teams is a complicated process. There are 31 **conferences** in the NCAA that automatically have one team qualify for the championship tournament. Every conference has its own tournament, and each winning team qualifies as one of the final 65 teams to play in the NCAA championship tournament. A committee selects the teams for the remaining 34 positions. They try to choose the country's best teams for the tournament.

The committee chooses two of the lowest ranked teams to play against each other. The winner of this game moves on to the first round of the championship. The committee arranges the teams in "the **bracket**." The bracket determines which teams will play each other based on region and rank.

The NCAA Men's Basketball Championship started out with eight teams competing in 1939. Today, 65 teams play in the championship.

UCLA has made it to the NCAA championships 43 times.

n the first round, there are four regional ournaments of 16 teams each. The four egions are East, West, South, and Midwest. In each region, the highest-ranked teams play against the owest-ranked teams. Once a eam loses a game, it is out of the competition. The winning teams move on to the next round.

There are 32 teams in the second round of the tournament. Each team plays another team, and the winners move on to the next round. Winners continue playing each other until here are only four teams left in the ournament. These four teams are he regional champions, and they play n the national semi-finals, known as he Final Four. The winners of this round play each other for the championship.

The Pittsburgh Panthers have played in the NCAA Championship 21 times.

The Net

Cutting down the net is an NCAA tradition for the championship team. Each player from the winning team cuts a piece of the basketball net. The coach cuts the last piece. Each player keeps a small piece of the net as a souvenir, and the coach keeps the rest.

Where They Play

With 10.8 seconds remaining in the game, fans watched as the Jayhawks tied the NCAA championship, forcing the game into overtime. They won the championship against Memphis.

The NCAA basketball championship game is a major event. Many cities compete for the opportunity to host the Final Four. Hosting the game brings many people to the city, boosting the city's economy by as much as $5 million. In 1987, 64,959 fans watched Indiana and Syracuse play in the championship game at the Louisiana Superdome in New Orleans. In 2008, more than 167,000 people took part in championship activities in San Antonio.

Mascots and cheerleaders perform in support of their team.

The host city is chosen a few years in advance of the game to give the city time to prepare for the big event. The host site must have a stadium that can seat 30,000 people. The city also must have a good transportation system and enough hotels to support the fans, teams, and officials.

While Ford Field in Detroit, Michigan, is actually football field, the center of the field was fitted with a basketball court for the 2008 NCAA Championship.

NCAA Championship Winners 2000–2009				
YEAR	**LOCATION**	**WINNING TEAM**	**SCORE**	**RUNNER-UP**
2009	Detroit	North Carolina	89–72	Michigan State
2008	San Antonio	Kansas	75–68	Memphis
2007	Atlanta	Florida	84–75	Ohio State
2006	Indianapolis	Florida	73–57	UCLA
2005	St. Louis	North Carolina	75–70	Illinois
2004	San Antonio	Connecticut	82–73	Georgia Tech
2003	New Orleans	Syracuse	81–78	Kansas
2002	Atlanta	Maryland	64–52	Indiana
2001	Minneapolis	Duke	82–72	Arizona
2000	Indianapolis	Michigan State	89–76	Florida

Mapping NCAA Champions

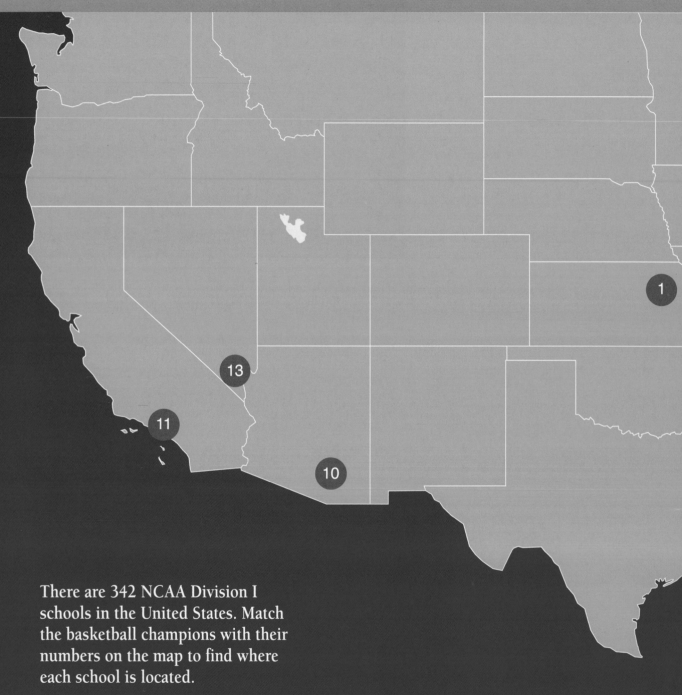

There are 342 NCAA Division I schools in the United States. Match the basketball champions with their numbers on the map to find where each school is located.

LEGEND

● NCAA Division I Champions

N
W — E
S

Scale

621 Miles

0   1,000 Kilometers

20

8

14

5

4

17

15

6

9

18

16

2

7   3

19

2

NCAA Division I Champions Since 1967

1) University of Kansas
2) University of Florida
3) University of North Carolina
4) University of Connecticut
5) Syracuse University
6) University of Maryland
7) Duke University
8) Michigan State University
9) University of Kentucky
10) University of Arizona

11) UCLA
12) University of Arkansas
13) UNLV
14) University of Michigan
15) Indiana University
16) University of Louisville
17) Villanova University
18) Georgetown University
19) North Carolina State University
20) Marquette University

Women and Basketball

At first, women's basketball was not a popular sport. In 1892, women's basketball had its own set of rules. Women played the first basketball tournament using men's basketball rules in 1926. The first five-player, full-court women's game was played in 1971.

In 1972, the government passed a law, called Title IX, that said schools had to fund men's and women's sports equally. As a result, women's sports programs began to grow. In 1978, the Association for Intercollegiate Athletics for Women (AIAW) televised their championship, and the Women's Basketball League (WBL), a women's professional league, was formed. The number of girls competing in high-school sports also increased. By 1972, about 2.7 percent of girls participated in school sports. Today, 40 percent of girls participate in school sports.

The AIAW ended in 1982, and the NCAA took control over women's collegiate sports. The first women's NCAA Division I tournament was in 1982. Interest in women's sports expanded, and women's basketball scholarships increased.

In the early years of the sport, women were required to wear floor length dresses when they played basketball.

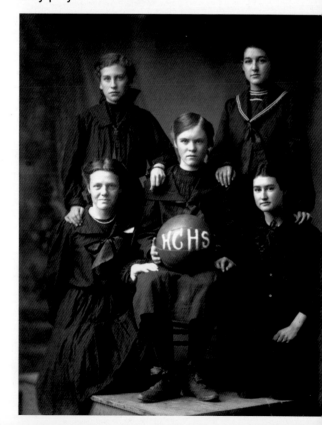

GET CONNECTED

Find more information about women's basketball at **www.wnba.com**.

Millions of fans watch the women's NCAA championship every year. The championship follows the same format as the men's tournament.

Women's basketball became very popular in the 1990s. The Women's National Basketball Association (WNBA) was formed in 1997. This organization gives top female college players the opportunity to play professional basketball in the United States.

Today, women's basketball follows the same rules as men's basketball. The only difference is that women use a smaller ball.

The New York Liberty played against the Los Angeles Sparks during the inaugural WNBA game in 1997. New York won 67 to 57.

Diana Taurasi

Diana Taurasi has one of the most successful college careers in women's basketball in the United States. She played for the University of Connecticut for four years, from 2000 to 2004, and her team won the NCAA championship three of those years. In college, Taurasi averaged 15 points, 4.5 assists, and 4.3 rebounds per game. She was named the Naismith National Player of the Year in 2003 and 2004. Taurasi was the first draft pick in the 2004 WNBA draft, and she currently plays for the Phoenix Mercury. In 2006, she was named the USA Basketball Female Athlete of the Year.

Historical Highlights

Some of the greatest basketball players in the world have played in the NCAA basketball championship. Throughout the history of the championship, some teams have led the tournament throughout the entire series, while other teams have come from behind to win the title. There have been nail-biting games that were won and lost in the final seconds.

Beginning in 1962, coach John Wooden led his UCLA team to 13 Final Four tournaments within 15 years, winning the championship 10 times. UCLA won the NCAA championship seven years in a row, from 1967 to 1973.

In 1979, Earvin "Magic" Johnson, playing for Michigan State, defeated Larry Bird and Indiana State in the NCAA championship. Almost 18 million people watched the game on television. It remains the highest-rated televised college game of all time. Magic Johnson and Larry Bird both went on to become NBA superstars.

In 1983, the North Carolina State Wolfpack played the University of Houston in the championship game. Houston was favored to win, and North Carolina was the **underdog**. In the final few seconds of the game, Lorenzo Charles of North Carolina made a surprise basket. He scored a **slam dunk**, and the Wolfpack won the game 54 to 52.

After Michigan state beat Indiana State, Magic Johnson was voted Most Outstanding Player of the Final Four for his extraordinary effort in the game.

In the championship game between Indiana and Syracuse in 1987, there were 28 seconds left in the game, and the score was 73 to 72 for Syracuse. Syracuse was closely guarding Indiana's strongest shooter, Steve Alford, so he could not get the ball and score. One of Keith Smart's teammates from Indiana saw that Smart was open on the baseline and passed him the ball. With four seconds left on the clock, Smart made the basket, and Indiana won the championship 74 to 73.

In the 2003 championship game, Kansas was down by three points to Syracuse. With only two seconds left in the game, Michael Lee of Kansas made a shot from the three-point line. However, Hakin Warrick of Syracuse blocked the ball and knocked it out of bounds. Syracuse won the game 81 to 78.

Keith Smart cut down part of the net after helping his team win the 1987 national title.

NCAA Championship Records

RECORD	PLAYER	TEAM	YEAR(S)
Points (44)	Bill Walton	UCLA	1973
Points by a Freshman (26)	Toby Bailey	UCLA	1995
Field Goals (21)	Bill Walton	UCLA	1973
Free Throws Made (18)	Gail Goodrich	UCLA	1965
Three-Pointers Made (7)	Steve Alford, Dave Sieger, Tony Delk	Indiana, Oklahoma, Kentucky	1987, 1988, 1996
Assists (11)	Rumeal Robinson	Michigan	1989
Rebounds (27)	Bill Russell	San Francisco	1956
Blocked Shots (6)	Joakim Noah	Florida	2006
Steals (7)	Tommy Amaker, Mookie Blaylock	Duke, Oklahoma	1986, 1988

LEGENDS and Current Stars

Michael Jordan

Wilt Chamberlain – Center

Wilt Chamberlain attended the University of Kansas, playing for the Jayhawks from 1956 to 1959. During his college career, he averaged 29.9 points and 18.3 rebounds per game. At 7 foot 1 inch (215 cm), the NCAA added rules so that Chamberlain did not have an advantage over other players. Chamberlain never won an NCAA championship. In his sophomore year, his team lost the championship in triple overtime. Although his team lost, Chamberlain was named the most valuable player (MVP) of the tournament. Chamberlain played professional basketball in the National Basketball Association (NBA) from 1959 to 1973. He won two NBA championships and set many records. In one game, he scored 100 points. This remains the highest individual score in NBA history.

Michael Jordan – Guard

Michael Jordan is one of basketball's most recognizable players. He played for the University of North Carolina Tar Heels from 1981 to 1984. As a freshman, Jordan was on the starting lineup, a rare accomplishment for a first-year student. Jordan is known for one of the most memorable moments in NCAA championship history. In the 1982 NCAA championship game, he made a **jump shot** in the last second of the game to defeat Georgetown University 63 to 62. After college, Jordan spent many years playing for the Chicago Bulls in the NBA. He led the Bulls to six NBA championships and won six MVP titles.

Wilt Chamberlain

Mario Chalmers

Mario Chalmers – Guard

Mario Chalmers played for the University of Kansas Jayhawks from 2005 to 2008. He helped lead his team to the NCAA championship title in 2008. In 2008, he was the Most Outstanding Player of the Final Four. Chalmers is an extraordinary defensive player. In his final year with the team, he had 97 steals and 169 assists. Chalmers is known for one of the most memorable plays in the NCAA championships. In the 2008 championship game against Memphis, he made a three-point shot with 2.1 seconds left, tying the game. His team then won in overtime. Chalmers joined the NBA in 2008 and currently plays for the Miami Heat.

Corey Brewer – Forward

Corey Brewer played for the University of Florida Gators from 2004 to 2007. He led his team to two NCAA championships in a row. Brewer is a strong defensive player. In the 2007 NCAA championship game against Ohio State, Brewer only allowed Ohio's star guard Ron Lewis to score 12 points. In that same game, Brewer scored 13 points and got 8 rebounds. Brewer was named the Most Outstanding Player of the NCAA Final Four in 2007. In his junior year, he was the Southeastern Conference's Defensive Player of the Year. Brewer joined the NBA in 2007 and plays for the Minnesota Timberwolves.

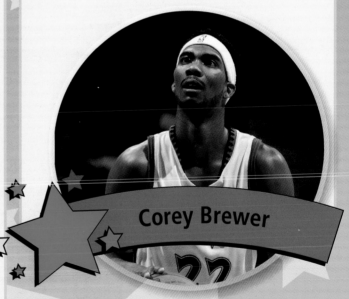

Corey Brewer

Famous Firsts

The term "March Madness" was first used in 1939 by H.V. Porter to describe the Illinois high school basketball finals. The term began to be used for the NCAA championship tournament in the 1980s.

In 1946, the championship game was televised for the first time. Oklahoma State defeated North Carolina, and the game was shown on New York local television. About 500,000 people watched the game. The championship game was televised nationally for the first time 1954.

In 1952, Seattle was the first city to host the Final Four, with the semi-finals and finals taking place in the same city.

In 1984, John Thompson, Jr. became the first African American coach to win the NCAA championship, when Georgetown University defeated Houston.

The University of Maryland became the first school to beat five former NCAA champions on their path to win the championship in 2002.

In 2004, the men's and women's teams from the University of Connecticut both won the NCAA championship. This was the first time that both the men's and women's teams from the same school won the title in the same year.

The first time the top four **seeded** teams made it to the Final Four was in 2008. The teams were Kansas, Memphis, UCLA, and North Carolina. Kansas won the championship.

In 1997, the University of Arizona was the first team to defeat three number one teams to win the championship.

The First Championship Game

The first NCAA championship game was held at the Patten Gymnasium in Evanston, Illinois, on March 27, 1939. Howard Hobson coached Oregon, which defeated Ohio State 46 to 43. Oregon dominated the rebounds and moved quicker down the court than Ohio State. John Dick from Oregon was the team's high scorer, with 13 points. About 5,500 people attended the game.

The Rise of the Championship

1891

Dr. James Naismith invents basketball.

1939

The first NCAA championship takes place. The University of Oregon wins the championship.

1946

Oklahoma State becomes the first team to win two championships in a row.

1953

The tournament expands from 16 to 22 teams.

1954

The NCAA championship game is televised nationally for the first time.

1966

Texas Western University, the first team with an all African American starting lineup, wins the championship.

1973

UCLA's coach John Wooden leads his team to the first of seven NCAA championship titles in a row. Thirty-nine million people watch the championship game on television.

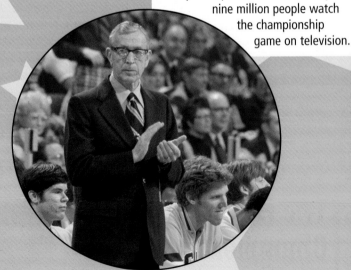

1975

The tournament expands to 32 teams.

1980

The tournament expands to 48 teams.

1984

The tournament expands to 53 teams.

1985

The tournament expands to 64 teams. Villanova, the eighth-seeded team, becomes the lowest-seeded team to ever win the NCAA championship.

1992

More than 34 million people watch Duke and Michigan play in the championship game.

2001

The tournament expands to 65 teams. Almost 16 million people watch the televised championship game.

QUICK FACTS

- Dr. Naismith also developed the basketball program at the University of Kansas.

- In 1950, City College of New York entered both the NIT and NCAA championships, and won both tournaments.

- The NCAA championship is also known as "The Big Dance."

Test Your Knowledge

1 Who invented basketball, and in what year?

2 Which was the first team to win the NCAA championship in 1939?

3 What is the highest-rated televised NCAA basketball game of all time?

4 How many NCAA Division I schools are there in the United States?

5 What university team did Michael Jordan play for?

6 How many referees are there in an NCAA basketball game?

7 Who was the first African American coach to win an NCAA championship?

8 Which NCAA basketball team has won the most championships?

9 Name one person who holds the record for most three-point shots made during an NCAA championship game.

10 Which is the lowest-seeded team to ever win the NCAA championship?

ANSWERS: 1.) Dr. James Naismith in 1891 2.) University of Oregon 3.) Michigan State and Magic Johnson against Indiana State and Larry Bird in 1979 4.) 342 5.) University of North Carolina Tar Heels 6.) Three 7.) John Thompson, Jr. 8.) UCLA has won the most championships. 9.) Steve Alford, Dave Sieger, and Tony Delk all made seven three-point shots in NCAA championship games. 10.) Villanova in 1985

Further Research

More information about basketball and the NCAA basketball championships can be found in books and on websites. To learn more about the NCAA, visit your library, or look online.

Books to Read

Search your library for books about the NCAA. On your library's computer, type in a keyword. The computer will help find information you are looking for. You can also ask a librarian for help.

Online Sites

The NCAA website contains a great deal of information about the sport and the championship tournament. You can find this website at **www.ncaa.com**.

Information about teams can be found on university and college websites. Check out **http://tarheelblue.cstv.com** to learn more about the Tar Heels. You also can type in the name of your favorite team on a search engine, such as Google.

To find out more about how March Madness works, visit **http://entertainment.howstuff works.com/march-madness.htm**.

Glossary

arced: curved, like an arch

bracket: a diagram showing a series of games in a tournament

circumference: the distance around an object

collegiate: having to do with college or college students

conferences: associations of sports teams that play against each other

defense: the team that is trying to keep another team from scoring

jump shot: a shot that is made while the player is jumping

offense: the team that has the ball and is trying to score points

prestigious: having high status and a good reputation

rebounding: bouncing the ball off the rim or the backboard

seeded: how a team is ranked in a tournament

slam dunk: a shot made when the player stuffs the ball through the basket

three-point line: a half circle around the center of the basket

underdog: the team with a disadvantage that is expected to lose

Index